21st Century
Junior Library

DISCOVER THE
APATOSAURUS

Lucia Raatma

Our Prehistoric World:
Dinosaurs

Published in the United States of America by:

CHERRY LAKE PRESS
2395 South Huron Parkway, Suite 200, Ann Arbor, Michigan 48104
www.cherrylakepress.com

Content Adviser: Gregory M. Erickson, PhD, Dinosaur Paleontologist, Department of Biological
Science, Florida State University, Tallahassee, Florida

Reading Adviser: Marla Conn, ReadAbility, Inc.

Photo and Illustration Credits: Cover: © Warpaint/Shutterstock.com; pages 5, 11: © Daniel Eskridge/
Shutterstock.com; page 6: © Ratpack2/Dreamstime.com; page 7: © schusterbauer.com/Shutterstock.com;
page 9: © danku/iStockphoto.com; page 10: © Mr1805/Dreamstime.com; page 12: © Gloda/iStockphoto.com;
pages 13, 20: © Elenarts/Shutterstock.com; page 14: © Linda Bucklin/Shutterstock.com; page 17:
© Daniel Eskridge/Dreamstime.com; page 18: © Eye Risk/Alamy; page 21: © ASSOCIATED PRESS

Cherry Lake Press is an imprint of Cherry Lake Publishing Group.

Library of Congress Cataloging-in-Publication Data has been filed and is available at catalog.loc.gov.

Cherry Lake Press would like to acknowledge the work of the Partnership for 21st Century Learning, a Network
of Battelle for Kids. Please visit http://www.battelleforkids.org/networks/p21 for more information.

Printed in the United States of America

Note from publisher: Websites change regularly, and their future contents are outside of our control.
Supervise children when conducting any recommended online searches for extended learning opportunities.

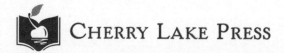

CHERRY LAKE PRESS

CONTENTS

WHAT WAS AN APATOSAURUS?

Imagine a dinosaur with a huge body. It has a small head and a long tail. That is an *Apatosaurus*. It lived about 150 million years ago. It was one of the largest land animals ever! Today, all types of dinosaurs are **extinct**.

The *Apatosaurus* was one of the largest animals of its time.

Some scientists believe the *Apatosaurus* is the same as the *Brontosaurus*. Scientists originally found two skeletons. They thought the skeletons were from different kinds of dinosaurs. So they gave each animal its own name.

Scientists believe *Apatosauruses* lived in groups.

Later, some said the skeletons were actually the same animal! *Apatosaurus* means "deceptive lizard." *Deceptive* means able to fool. Today, scientists once again say they are two species.

WHAT DID AN APATOSAURUS LOOK LIKE?

The *Apatosaurus* was big. It was 70 to 90 feet (21 to 27 meters) long. The top of its back was around 15 feet (4.6 m) high. The *Apatosaurus* could hold its head about 17 feet (5.2 m) high. The dinosaur weighed around 30 tons. That's about as much as three school buses!

An *Apatosaurus* had a long neck and tail.

The *Apatosaurus*'s head was very small compared to its body.

The *Apatosaurus* was huge, but its head was small. In fact, its head was only about 2 feet (0.6 m) long. Its brain was about the size of an apple. Its teeth were like little pencils. This dinosaur had **nostrils** on top of its head. No one is sure why its nostrils were located there.

Look!

Stand in front of a full-length mirror. Look at the size of your head. Now compare it to the size of your whole body. That huge *Apatosaurus* sure had a tiny head!

It would be dangerous to be caught under an *Apatosaurus*'s heavy legs.

Create!

Go into your yard or a nearby park. Take a tape measure with you. Measure around the trunks of a few trees. Make a chart that compares the smallest to the largest. Imagine how big an *Apatosaurus*'s leg was!

The *Apatosaurus* had thick, heavy legs. Each one was about the size of a large tree trunk. This dinosaur had tough skin, which helped protect it from predators. It had a long neck. Its long tail could whip back and forth.

The *Apatosaurus* might have stood on its back legs to reach treetops.

14

HOW DID AN APATOSAURUS LIVE?

The *Apatosaurus* was an **herbivore**. That means it ate only plants. It **grazed** on ferns, bushes, sticks, tree leaves, and pine cones. Its long neck helped it reach into a **grove** of trees to feed. However, its neck was not like a giraffe's. It reached forward, not up into the air.

How much do you chew your food before swallowing? The *Apatosaurus* did not chew at all! It ate its food whole. It also swallowed rocks to help **digest** the food. As the dinosaur moved around, the rocks bounced in its stomach. Its stomach also churned, or moved, the food. This helped break down the food.

Make a Guess!

How big do you think the rocks were that an *Apatosaurus* ate? Do you think they were little stones? Or were they big boulders? Make a guess. Ask a parent, teacher, or librarian for help finding the answer. Did you guess correctly?

Rocks helped an *Apatosaurus* digest food as the dinosaur moved around.

The *Apatosaurus* could use its tail like a whip to hit enemies.

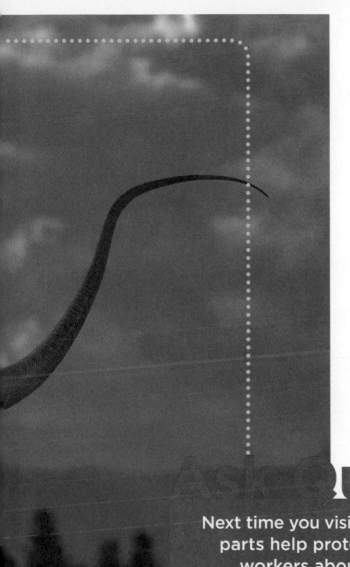

Can you picture a huge creature plodding along? That's what the *Apatosaurus* did. It moved slowly on its heavy feet. To protect itself, it would swing its heavy tail around. This helped keep meat-eating dinosaurs away.

Ask Questions!

Next time you visit a zoo, look at the animals. What body parts help protect them from other animals? Ask zoo workers about how your favorite animal stays safe.

The *Apatosaurus* lived in the western areas of North America. How do we know? Scientists have found its fossils in Colorado and other western states. The fossil of one *Apatosaurus* is on display in Pittsburgh, Pennsylvania. By studying fossils, scientists can learn about how dinosaurs lived.

This scientist is studying the fossils of a young *Apatosaurus*.

GLOSSARY

digest (dye-JEST) to break down food so the body can use it

extinct (ek-STINGKT) describing a type of plant or animal that has completely died out

fossils (FAH-suhlz) the preserved remains of living things from thousands or millions of years ago

grazed (GRAYZD) fed on low-growing plants

grove (GROHV) a group of trees growing together

herbivore (UR-buh-vor) an animal that eats plants rather than other animals

nostrils (NOSS-truhlz) the opening through which air passes when an animal smells or breathes

predators (PRED-uh-turz) animals that live by hunting other animals for food

FIND OUT MORE

Books

Braun, Dieter. *Dictionary of Dinosaurs: An Illustrated A to Z of Every Dinosaur Ever Discovered.* New York, NY: Chartwell Books, 2022.

Mara, Wil. *Apatosaurus.* New York, NY: Children's Press, 2012.

Websites

With an adult, learn more online with these suggested searches.

American Museum of Natural History: Fossil Halls—Apatosaurus
Read about the *Apatosaurus* fossil on exhibit.

Carnegie Museum of Natural History: Dinosaurs in Their Time
Learn about all sorts of dinosaurs at this museum.

INDEX

ABOUT THE AUTHOR

Lucia Raatma has written dozens of books for young readers. She and her family live in the Tampa Bay area of Florida. They enjoy looking at the dinosaur fossils at the local science museum.